My love for you, inside the circle,
It's like a ring of fire, burning,
Strong, pure and kind, eternal,
Each day, each night and morning.

RING OF FIRE

Poems

BY MARIUS ALEXANDRU

RING OF FIRE

Poems

BY MARIUS ALEXANDRU

My love for you, inside the circle, It's like a ring of fire, burning,
Strong, pure and kind, eternal, Each day, each night and morning

Table of Contents

A Divine Essence

Love is a flower spreading beautiful perfume

a divine essence

A Drop of Heaven

It's raining on people with angels and flowers, and I am dancing with the stars,

A drop of Heaven dripped into my soul.

A love that's paying any price

She always has a special way of showing her great love,

Her love for me is here to stay, Like blessings pouring from above.

A love that's paying any price, A love that will hold true,

A love that's kind, and sacrifices… And for that love, MOM, I love you!

A Mother is a Song

A Mother is a song and flower,

She's the hand that caresses when it hurts, A Mother is a tear falling to the ground, and is the holiest word in the world.

A Mother is the ray of sunshine and light, mysterious balm that soothes,

A Mother is an angel sent from heaven,

A Mother is the good-fairy from the dream.

A Mother is "Doina" a Mother is "Dor", A Mother is hope, faith, help,

A Mother is a smile and the clear sky, A Mother is the altar of eternal love.

A Mother is the clear blue sea,

A Mother is a muse, and she is a verse of poetry, On life's painting, a Mother is a color,

A Mother is an eternal holiday.

A Mother is clean spring water,

A Mother is a white wing in flight, A Mother is a trill of a skylark,

A Mother is a wonderful melody.

A Mother is a sweet breeze,

A Mother is the most sacred covenant,

A Mother is what's the best, dearest, and most beautiful, A Mother carries in her, the image of Christ!

A Test

Tied to the earth With heavy chains Started at birth

With smiles and pains Please free my soul My caged heart

Life takes its toll It takes its part

But soon the death Will solve my quest

As I will take New Life's breath A test

Tied to the earth With twisted ropes Genuine mirth

Lost dreams, new hopes Putrid smell

New songs Tales to tell

Rights and wrongs But soon untied Free, I will rest

When I will watch the New Sunrise A test

Tied to the earth

By unknown powers A mighty girth

Doubtful passing hours Amazing nights

Dreary mornings Hollow lights Seemly adornings I'll fly through skies Here I'm a guest My soul never dies A test

A Thousand Years

I believe in love and in miracles,

I believe in spring's rain and rainbows, I believe in prophecies and oracles,
But I'm afraid of time and shadows.

When I think of you when I see your tears, When in my dreams I can hear
your laughter, I am full of hope, my fear disappears,

A thousand years before, a thousand years after.

Dying a little bit each day I fully live, Thinking that soon I'll be close to you
again, A thousand years is all I have to give,

To kiss your hair, to walk with you in the rain.

I have always believed in our strong love, There is nothing that can separate
us, Your eyes are shining in the stars above, I'll love you for a thousand
years and, plus.

All I Want is Here with Me

All I want is the sparkles from your eyes, in the cold days of winter,

Your smile in the early mornings of spring,

All I want is the same flame we started thirty summers ago, All I want is blue butterflies to fly and golden birds to sing.

I want the leaves you softly walk on,

I want to hear your whispers in the fall, I want your hand walking the alleys,

I want your heart, your soul, your… all.

I want the lilies from your shiny hair, and the roses from your lips,

I want your breath, I want your touch,

I want your rest, your dream, your sleep.

I want your laughter, and your cry,

To kiss your cheeks when tears run down, I want the sun, the moon, the sky,

I want your love… the greatest crown.

All I want is here with me,

I cannot put in rhyme, your worth, But I can tell you; I love thee,

I'm blessed… the happiest man on Earth.

All the time in the world

All the time in the world

is not enough for our love,

Cannot be fitted in this space, cannot be curled in a finite, limited, small clove.

Seconds, minutes, hours, years, decades, are not enough to kiss your eyes,

Our love will live forever in the sacred shades, in twinkling lights flying through the skies.

I know that hundreds of thousands of years

are not enough to listen to your girlish laughter, to watch your smiles, to wipe your tears,

I'll need the eternity and the ever after!

Amazing Grace-Rondelet

Amazing Grace

Always with me in this hard ride Amazing Grace

Soon I will see You face to face Soon we'll be standing side by side

You, my sweet Groom, and I, Your Bride Amazing Grace.

Another Year with You

Another year is coming,

The old one, like a whisper, flew, Please, make me Lord more loving, In this New Year, with You!

Another year, another race,

We walk together stride by stride, In every step I feel Your Grace, You're always by my side.

Another year of mercies, Poured over me each day, A year of peace, no worries, Because You are The Way!

Another year is coming,

So many dreams I will pursue, I do not know Your timing, Another year with You!

Anticipation

Abide in Me, The Lord had said Apart from Me is pain and strife Amazing Grace, I raised the dead Accept My gift, eternal life.

Atonement

Acquitted, forever forgiven

A Love that I will never understand Absolved and destined for Heaven Always, by Grace kept in Your hand. Affirm

Appraised as "not worthy" Assessed "with no value" Abysmal, filthy and dirty Anything good I can't do Aught

Anomaly, You, died for me

Articulating, without the words, Your Love Attesting that I'm yours, and free Awaiting for my home, above

Anticipation

Apart

Walking the bridge of the unknown, Suspended between earth and heaven,

So many mermaids swimming in the skies, and angels flying in the seas,

The only light it's in her eyes, She put my heart at ease.

I walk the pier of the unknown,

I hear the silence talking… she's so loud So many dreams remain unborn,

So many roses without a thorn. Where is the end? When did I start? So many questions still unanswered, I ask the shadows of my heart,

How long, how long we'll stay apart?

Blue Bird

I turned to blue because I'm happy,

I carry deep in my small heart

the taste of freedom and the skies. Sweet little girl, can't you see?

I turned to blue, like your blue eyes.

I simply wanted to be like you, Pure, kind without worries,

I thought that's something I can do, So this morning in a hurry,

I kiss your eyes and turned to blue.

Blue Butterflies

Golden dust   of the moon
shifts musical notes,   Blue butterflies
  are carpet for the   forest, The stars
    crack come down to my   OO   OO   table in the evening,
    It's a happy and beautiful   \   /   world... in my dreams.
    It snows upside down with   \ /   white snowdrops kissing
    the red sun's rays, Silky flakes **sing,** the silver bells ring, it is a
    cleaner and better world in my dreams. Tears turned into dew
    on the still unborn grass beneath my feet, The yellow birds
      fly towards the light, and the flowers smell of joy, It is
        peace, and quiet and harmony in my dreams
        Cherry blossoms dance as the angels sing the
        violin, It is a big holiday every day, It is eternal
        Spring... in my   dreams. Golden dust of the
        moon shifts   musical notes, Butterflies
          are carpet for   the   forest, The
            stars crack   come down
              to my   table...

Marius Alexandru

Chains

I like to break those heavy chains, Which keeps me tied to earth,

And free… to fly released from pains, To my new life, to my new birth.

To wander, peacefully through the stars,

-A magical journey above-

And happily, to leave these shores, To meet my Prince, to meet my Love.

Cherry blossom rise

Cherry blossom rise Snowdrops announce the Spring's birth

Winter slow resigns

Childhood

Childhood is a beautiful dream that never disappears, A world of wonders often recaptured in memories,

A time without worries, just smiles, beauty, and color,

We all find ourselves in it, the heroes of the most beautiful story.

Childhood is the laughter, the games,

The start of everything, purest spring of our souls,

A halt in life, a stop where for a moment everyone descends,

A magical universe, decorated with silver stars and blue flowers.

Childhood is a sunray of hope in the muddy road, A tear drowned in laughter,

A wind that spreads around the smell of lime, perfume Childhood is spring rain, a smile in the mirror.

Christmas Eve

It's snowing beautifully outside, crystals are flying everywhere, The streets are covered in bright white, and love is in the air, Frozen windows, tremble when happy carolers are passing by, White angels, disguised in soft flakes are dancing in the sky.

I'm snuggled up, all warm and cozy by my fireplace, inside,

The sound of burning wood… a melody so peacefully, so sublime, I'm reading The Christmas Story, by the candlelight,

A smiling star, waving at me, whispers… good night, good night…

Courage

Bent in the grand dance of the red poppies, We let our courage rise from this seeded field, We feed it with the truth of yesterday's glories, Our history, our sword, our shield.

Where slumber squeezes the lost dreams, New hopes have born in us the faith again, Awakened, our conscience cries and screams, We walk barefooted, free in the rain.

The eternal wild of child and happiness, Fresh grass, blue skies, no worries,

A little touch of tenderness,

We write with red our new stories.

Dreaming pure thoughts that change the world, Caring and loving, praying and singing,

Living our life for our country and the Lord, Whatever comes, in the end, we're winning!

Covid Acrostic

C hrist alone can stop the fear **O**nly He can give us peace **V**iruses, sickness will reappear **I**n our world, year after year **D**ecay, death will never cease.

Daddy's Hands

strong, powerful hands

love and blessings touch my head happy father's day

Dancing on the Sheet Music

The low musical notes on the staff think of themself very highly,

and the high notes, are losing their heads over the top,

but from time to time they meet humbly in the middle,

such a strange harmony.

Daydreaming

White winter blankets cover the earth, Unseen angels transcend through universes, carrying prayers on their wings.

Cadences we don't understand turns into lyrics. We dream with open eyes, again.

Deception

From a distance, the stars were so beautiful, Red, white and pink.

They smelled like roses.

They fell on earth, melted and start to stink.

Delightful Morning

honey sunshine rays

a sweet kiss to my coffee delightful morning

Divine Face

On the glimmers of water, I see Your Divine face, You decorate the ocean, coral after coral, You are in the smallest sand grain, Grace,

And I feel Your presence in every wave, Immortal.

Divine Love

Candles burning, Tears drop melting, Soul lost, no hope. Cold stars crying, Wilted flowers lying, Ending rope.

Coldest nights, Lost rights, Rusted chains. Prison walls, Missing calls, Fear reigns.

Violent storms, Shadows, ghosts, forms Terrible scare.

Secret whispers, Deadly twisters, Chilly air.

Blurry mornings, Broken wings, Painful cage.

Vexing nightmares, Unanswered prayers, Unending rage.

Red fresh roses, Fragrant posies, Infinite tenderness. Different man, Born again,

Eternal happiness. Light revealed, New war field, Shining star.

Dreams restored, Fighting sword, Lighting far.

Rivers flowing, Bluebirds singing, Faith renewed.

Smiling Sun, Freedom won,

Love, Thanksgiving, Gratitude. Dep, deep oceans,

Pure emotions, Gentle dove. Hope regained, Life reclaimed, Divine Love.

Dream

I made for myself wings from faith and love I wanted to fly like a white dove

I wanted to kiss the blue sky to smile at clouds passing by I wanted to roam free

to cry with the sea I wanted peace wars to cease

I scream Dream

The poem consists of 10 lines, rhyme, tells a story, and counts down from ten syllables to one.

The EXTREME part of this format is that the poem can be read from line 10 to 1, or from line 1 to 10, and it will flow and make sense in either direction.

Dreaming of Spring

Golden dust of the moon sifts musical notes, Blue butterflies are carpet for the forest,

The stars crack come down to my table in the evening, It's a happy and beautiful world... in my dreams.

It snows upside down with white snowdrops kissing the red sun's rays, Silky flakes sing, the silver bells ring,

It's a cleaner and better world... in my dreams.

Tears turned into dew on the still unborn grass beneath my feet, The yellow birds fly towards the light, and the flowers smell of joy, It's peace, and quiet and harmony... in my dreams.

Cherry blossom dance as the angels sing the violin,

It's a big holiday every day, it's eternal Spring... in my dreams.

Easter Morning

Easter morning has arrived, the greatest time to show your love, In the church the kids are singing, angels smile from above.

Please, remember to forgive as your sins were once forgiven, You're called to live for Him, His will on Earth as it is in Heaven!

If you're sorry start repenting, say a prayer from your heart,

He will hear you and forgive you, as His Children you're set apart.

Our Father is so pleased when we live for Him with passion, Watching from His home to us give Him so much satisfaction.

Lost in the night the world was waiting for this morning to arrive, With my mother, both we're singing; He has risen! He's alive!

On my street the trees are dancing, happiness is all around, Hallelujah, Christ has risen! Christ has risen a sweet sound!

Sunday Morning has arrived, the greatest time to show your love, In the Church the kids are singing, angels smile from above.

Easter-Cinquain

Easter Joyful, victorious

Rebirth, rejuvenation, revival, Coming back to Life Resurrection

Endless Summer

Endless summer, Millions of stars, blue butterflies,

Endless summer, dancing happy with my lover,

I smell the rain I close my eyes, I feel his lips, sweet paradise, Endless summer.

Eternal bliss

Your every hug and every kiss, It's like a gift, eternal bliss,

Sometimes at night, I watch your sleep, An innocent and lovely peep,

I'm grateful for you to God above,

I whisper; I love you my wife, my love!

Eternity Gate

freedom for my soul the time ceases to exist eternity gate

Faith-Cinquain

Faith Confidence, assurance Walking without seeing

Inspiring trust absolute sublime Conviction

Far Away

We hugged each other, overwhelmed with grace, Oh, how I long for that safe, happy place,

To kiss your lips, to touch your lovely face.

You are so far away yet next to me,

Between us are high mountains, the deep sea, My love for you knocked all the shackles free.

Fields of Love

blossom of red fires

the graceful poppies dancing fields of love and hope

Fighting Fear

Fighting fear, we gain courage, strength, and confidence,

we learn by living (paraphrasing Eleanor Roosevelt)

Forever Kid

I don't think being an adult is going to work for me…

I don't want to give up flying with the butterflies in the sun,

I don't want to give up romping with the lambs on the plains,

I don't want to give up singing with the birds or jumping with the bees from flower to flower, I don't want to give up dreaming of white angels and pink fairies,

I don't want to give up believing in Santa.

I don't think being an adult is going to work for me.

Friendship

This means to tend and to be kind,

To see through the eyes of your friend, To imperfections to be blind,

To care and love until the end.

This is the most amazing sight,

His tears to flow like rivers in your eyes, To make his worries your own fight,

To fly together through the skies.

Goodbye

"I'm going away tonight." (James Brown) "I've said all that I've had to say." (Bill Hicks) I wrote all that I've had to write

There's no reason for me to stay.

I will not have any last words

"Last words are for fools who haven't said enough." (Karl Marx) I'm looking forward to my heaven's awards

Let me fly, open my earthly handcuffs.

"Applaud my friends, the comedy is finished." (Ludwig Van Beethoven)

"I have fought the good fight, I have finished the race, I have kept the faith." (Apostle Paul) Everything seems so short… a minute

I tried to do all that God saith.

I hear so close, the final call,

"Tomorrow, at sunrise, I shall no longer be here." (Nostradamus) "You're right. It's time. I love you all." (Michael Landon)

I will be gone… but I'll be near.

Based on the last words heard from, or written by famous people.

Grace after Grace

I was lost.

I was wandering the dark streets of my soul taking my sacrifice on cold, fireless altars,

But God sought me with His love that never falters,

He found me through His Son, Jesus, and made me whole.

He took me in His arms.

At the cross, He hugged me and loved me, He gave me a new life, as a gift,

I was blind, and now I see,

And since then I walk hand in hand with Him, happy in His fullness and… grace after grace.

Happy Birthday, honey!

I'm blessed to have you in my life,

Your care fills up my days with pleasure, I'm thankful that you are my wife,

Your love for me, I treasure.

We walked together one more mile, With you the darkest days are sunny,
You bring me joy with your sweet smile, I love you! Happy Birthday, honey!

Heroes

My silent tears kissed the pure, white snowdrops and changed them into scarlet poppies,

so I will never forget your sacrifices.

His Bride

We will see Jesus at midnight, Be like a watchman on the wall,

And woe to you if you're not right, Soon we will hear the trumpet call.
We're looking forward to the ride, The Groom will take away His Bride.

Pain, sorrows you will face ahead, This world is blinded by the Lie,

But words of courage we can spread, Because we're looking at the sky.

We'll soon be standing by His side, The Groom will take away His Bride.

Hope-Triolet

Lost in the Winter's coldest night, My soul is singing songs of Spring. I dream of colors sun and light.

Lost in the Winter's coldest night,

I look with hope beneath the white, And happy never cease to sing.

Lost in the Winter's coldest night, My soul is singing songs of Spring.

Hope

This bitter world carries its darkness, The sky is sad and black, and starless

Forgotten in the forest, the moon is crying, Our hope is slowly dying.

It rises, once part of us but not anymore, In vain we knock on heaven's door,

It seems nobody's there to open,

I wonder if we'll be forever broken?

Nothing can prepare you for the future, You have to see the bigger picture,

The hope must be again revived,

The Light of the World, The Hope arrived!

Fumbling with something unfinished,

It makes somehow His Love diminished, Sometimes is peace, and
sometimes strife, But trust in Him with your whole life!

Hope-Cinquain

Hope Desire, wait

Looking with expectation Optimistic in future fulfilments Promise

Hugged

I caught in my cold palms

the sparkles of love from the tears of your pure eyes. I wanted you to stay here, never to leave,

embraced forever to hide in the lights.

I squeezed slightly to my chest your soft body as a flower, I wanted you to stay here, an eternity, always with me, hugged to spread our fragrance to the sun.

I touched with my red and warm cheek your cheek white and soft, I understood right away, right there, that

I was going to bathe my whole life in the waters of love which I found in your sweet whispers.

I wiped away the tears, the nectar of suffering, and I freed your smile to fly.

We stayed there together, daily overwhelmed with grace. We hugged, and slowly we start to walk toward our last Call.

Humility-Cinquain

Humility Modesty, compassion

Properly placed confidence Being free from pride Candor

I am a broken vessel

I am a broken vessel before You,

The hot tears of my soul pour on Your holy feet,

pure mirth, my prayers without words, my trembling heart.

My knees bend and fall to the ground, In my dirty hand, the towel shakes,

I am afraid, I am frightened, I am crying and hopeless, But from the cross, Grace smiles at me.

You sacrificed Yourself for me again, today You made my sigh a new song,

You made me Your beloved son, Your peace surrounds me,

The hot tears of my soul pour on Your holy feet,

pure mirth, my prayers without words, my trembling heart.

I am a Lighthouse

I am a Lighthouse, proud and tall, ignoring all the waves, Inside the chambers of my soul is peace,

I do not care how badly the stormy sea behaves, His songs of love and mercies never cease.

My Keeper helps me daily my Light is always on,

My eyes have seen the glory of the resurrected Lord, In the darkest hour, right before the dawn,

The mighty storm is silent at His majestic Word,

I warn so many ships at sea of the great danger, I show the Light, the safety to the port,

I guide them to The One born in a manger,

To the Truth, the Way, the Life, the strongest Fort,

I am a Lighthouse standing on the Rock of Ages, The Light for all that hopelessly roam,

Hope in all the storm that rages,

I safely lead the sailors to the Home.

I
am a poet*!*

The
lyrics
are the
tender
whispers
of love…
Poetry is
the life of
the poet,
his soul,
h*i*s
impr*i*nt,
/
/
a
journey,
a flight, a
trail on the
sheet of life.
I write because
I live. I am a poet!

Marius Alexandru

I am a small Light

My eyes have seen the glory of the resurrected Lord,

My ears have heard the Story, By grace, I am restored!

My eyes have seen the Light and everything is new,

No more darkness, no more night, I am a small light too.

I'll shine my light to the world, I would not hide in fear,

I will proclaim Your Word, Your love for all to hear.

I am a small light in a stand, My life is lighting the sky,

And soon I'll be at His Right Hand, The Child of The-Most-High!

I'm Yours

I'm yours before the time, Before I even said I do,

I'm yours, and you are mine, Forever, I love you!

I am the shore,

You are the wind, the wave I'm thirsty for your touch, All night your love I crave.

I am the sky at dawn,

You are the sun, ready to rise, I feel your soft and tender lips kissing my eyes.

I am a snowdrop,

and you are the Spring, For you, I live,

to you, I cling.

I'm yours before the time, Before I even said I do,

I'm yours, and you are mine, Forever, I love you!

I did not Die

It's not a time to weep and mourn, I hear so loud and clear the gong,

I have to go it is my turn,

Through the stars, I'll wear my song.

Why should your heart be broken, sad when I walk on pearled streets together with mom and dad,

and sit with Kings on golden seats?

The black earth did not swallow me, It's not a time for tears, don't cry,

I am with angels, flying free I am alive I did not die.

My Groom is carrying me in His arms, Dressed in white, His lovely Bride,

Each morning glows with heavenly charms, I did not die I'm by His side.

Is not adieu it's just goodbye, We'll meet again I did not die.

I Freed your Smile

I caught in my cold palms

the sparkles of love from the tears of your pure eyes. I wanted you to stay here, never to leave,

embraced forever to hide in the lights.

I squeezed slightly to my chest your soft body as a flower, I wanted you to stay here, an eternity, always with me, hugged to spread our fragrance to the sun.

I touched with my red and warm cheek your cheek white and soft, I understood right away, right there, that

I was going to bathe my whole life in the waters of love which I found in your sweet whispers.

I wiped away the tears, the nectar of suffering, and I freed your smile to fly.

I knew that we will grow old together

It was a summer day with blue, clear skies, When I saw first time your gentle smile,

Instantly, I was in love with your brown, sparkly eyes, I was in awe, I paused to breathe for a while.

I knew right away, right there, that you are the one, I knew that we will grow old together,

I knew that our time has just begun, And that we'll live as one, forever.

You are my gift from God above,

You took my heart with just a glance, I was enslaved by your great love,

There stood our genuine, pure romance.

We started our happy, exciting, eventful journey And every morning we retake it from the beginning,

I find new powers in your warm caress and your presence next to me, In any circumstances and hard times, our love I know is winning.

You are my muse in everything I do and write, You are a pleasant thrill in all my thoughts,

You are my pains, my sorrow, my happiness, and my delight You are the shining star in my darkest nights.

It was a summer day with blue, clear skies, My heart was burning in the hot weather

Instantly, I was in love with your brown, sparkling eyes, I knew that we will grow old together.

I listened to Silence

I stopped and listened to silence, and I heard the angels singing Hallelujah,

I closed my eyes,

and I saw the Star shining Love.

I Love my City

As all the bright, bright city lights, Extinguished one by one,

I watched in awe the city sights, A day just had begun.

With my eyes closed, I feel the sun, It raises once again,

I want to cry, to sing, to run, I want to hug the rain.

I hear the waves crashing the shore, Such music to my ears,

A symphony that I adore, I'm lost in childish tears.

I walk alone by "Lake Shore Drive" Chicago never sleeps,

My city is awake, alive Chicago is for keeps.

I love you… my love!

A hundred hearts would be too few, To carry all my love for you,

Oceans and seas are not enough, To fill my love would be so tough!

My waves of love will never end, I'll always follow the same trend,

Like teenagers, I'll carve your name

in every tree. My love for you I'll proclaim.

Each morning when I see your smile,

Is like the first day when I walked the aisle, And when I look into your eyes,

I see the stars lighting the skies.

During the day I hold your hand, You are my Queen from a fairyland, I walk with you year after year,

And heaven starts for us right here.

In evenings, when we're laughing free, I'm happy that you're next to me,

And every hug and every kiss, It's like a gift, eternal bliss.

Sometimes at night, I watch your sleep, An innocent and lovely peep,

Grateful for you to God above,

I whisper; I love you… my wife, my love!

I love you

If I were a tear,

I would bathe naked in your eyes, in the ocean of your pure love,

If I were a smile,

I would rest happily in the corner of your lips, holding to that place forever,

If I were a flower,

I would bloom in your chestnut, curly hair touching your velvety white cheek.

If I where the sun,

I would paint rainbows on every one of your tears, and if I were a star, I would descend from above to meet the light of your eyes.

If I were a wave,

I would bring you pearls from the bottom of the ocean, and if I were the breeze, I would whisper slowly,

in the coolness of the morning, I Love You.

I Miss You, Daddy!

I miss your tender call,

Your pleasant voice of the father,

I miss you to pick me up when I fall, I miss all the time spent together.

I miss your parental advice, I miss your wise words,

I miss you teaching me how to be nice, And how to fly free like the wildest birds.

I miss you telling me that I was wrong,

But also that is normal to make some mistakes, I miss you telling me; be strong,

You son, have got what it takes!

I miss you walking me to school, I miss playing together,

I miss you placing in my hand first tool,

I miss you. I miss you so much, my dear father!

I miss the evenings waiting for you to come from work, I miss reading from the scriptures,

I miss your stories that were scattering the dark,

I miss all the memories, all the black-and-white, old pictures.

I miss you praying with me,

Holding my hand, both of us kneeling, Nobody took care of me like thee,

I miss you, a bittersweet feeling.

I miss your laughter I miss your tears,

I miss the good days and the hardest ones too, I miss you sometimes pulling my ears,

I love you, Daddy, I'll always miss you!

I miss so many unspoken words, So many things that I failed to see,

I miss the Easter and Christmas cards,

I miss you, Daddy, but you're always with me!

I saw You this morning

I saw You this morning in the sunrise, Through the sunrays, You whispered to me; Everything that's in front of your eyes,

It's just for you; the mountains, the valleys… the sea.

I heard You this morning in wave after wave, In the beautiful song of the birds flying,

I knew right away that, next to You I'll be strong and brave, I lost forever, my strange old fear of dying.

I glanced a second through the curtain, I saw the tree of life, I smelled its fruits,

I smelled the perfume of lilies, in the garden, I dreamt about my glorious roots.

I felt You in the breeze, that was gently touching my cheeks, You hugged me, once again with love,

I was amazed, I couldn't move, I couldn't speak, But I had wings, I flew and touched the stars above.

I taste Your goodness every day, I see the beauty on Your face,

You are The Life, You are The Way, You cover me with Love and Grace!

I See The Light

In the world of dark and silence, At the edge of the abyss,

I'm waiting for my cruel sentence, Trapped between the whispers of pain, and a touch of bliss.

I sit alone dreaming of light.

Grayish angels of the unknown talk with me, without a word,

Choirs are singing melodies without a tone, Scouring the skies flies a frightened bird.

I'm lost alone in the night. The silence is so strong I cry

I pray to God for just a Word, I know I sinned and I must die, Have mercy, please, my Lord!

In the night, I See The Light!

In the world of light and praises, At the edge of Paradise,

Sitting on The Rock of Ages, I'm free again I lost my pains, You paid the price.

I walk with You in The Eternal Light!

I See the Shore

When the storms of life are raging, When the winds so angry roar,

On Your promises, I'm standing, Trusting You, I see the shore.

Oh, sweet Jesus, help me carry, All my burdens until the end, Take away all of my worries, All my pains to You I send.

In obedience, I will follow You, whatever comes my way,

Happiness or sometimes sorrow, Long dark nights or sunny days.

Yes! You promised that You'll hold me, And no one can make me harm, There's no force, and never will be, Strong enough to break Your hand.

Who can ever keep me distant From Your never-ending love?

On the cross, You made the payment, My freeway to Heaven above.

Safely covered by Your Grace,

I might walk here, a few more years, Soon I'll see You... face to face,

And You'll wipe away my tears.

I Stopped to Paint and Dance

It's snowing beautifully outside,

I stopped to paint with yellow, blue, black and white, over the frozen branches,

and with the snowflakes, together we start to dance in the light.

I Won't Let Go

Two immortal spirits, growing apart in smoke and flame, just to be reunited forever into eternal life.

Two lovers disappearing into dust after the game, of unaccepted love, bleeding under butcher's knife.

Two lonely souls wandering in the abyss, dreaming about the light, and wings, and stars, reliving, again and again, their last kiss, forgetting that they wear so many scars.

If

If I were a composer, I would write musical notes in a bouquet, and I would lay it down at your feet in a beautiful song,

If I were a painter, I would paint on the canvas, red butterfly the colors of love, If I could fly, I would pick up for you a bunch of shining stars,

and I would make the sunrise a special gift for you in the morning. I would put the rainbow at your feet,

and I would shout out my love for you from the top of the mountains in the echo. But I soak my pen in love and through the verses, I sign; I Love You!

I hold you in my arms, full of happiness, once again,

and I give you a rose, together with my whole life, forever, my love.

Innocence

Planted in God's garden, By the River of Love, Breathing Grace,

Bloomed to whisper Spring is here.

It Was a Dark and Stormy Night

It was a dark and stormy night, When God has given us The Light!

Jeremiah 29: 11-14

For I know the plans I have for you declares The Lord at the beginning,

I am, The One, I can, I'll do

in the New Year, a brand-new meaning,

For I know the plans I have for you, Plans for good and plans to prosper, I'll give you hope a future too,

I am your God I am your Father,

When you'll call upon My Name

with your full heart, when you'll seek Me, I will wash away your shame,

You will live forever, free

All my promises I will fulfill

I will give you blessings, every day I love you I always will,

In this New Year, with you, I'll stay!

Kneeling at The Cross

I have stilled and quieted my soul, I listened to the whispers of pain,

I closed my eyes so I could see heaven crying, I opened my arms to receive Your hug,

and I fell to my knees, at The Cross, overwhelmed with Love.

Knees of clay pray in silence

Knees of clay pray in silence, On the altar, the heart is burning.

Released... the tear from the eyelids, it flies with the songs of my soul, to the heights of Infinite Light.

Lessons

When you're deep in the dark valleys, Full of hope look to the Lord,

Just remember the old rallies... It waits for you a new reward.

When you're walking on the mountains of success and many blessings,

On your most amazing day,

Learn from life's valuable lessons, Humbly kneel down, humbly pray.

Life is But a Dream

I searched the world over

hoping to find my true love once again,

I ran in the dreaming to rediscover the mystic garden, where my lover used to hold my hand in the rain.

I was alone, nobody near, The time had come to a stop,

A mighty wind blew in the fear, Shadows of discouragement appear, My tears and the rain, drop after drop.

Guilty thoughts could not erase my memories of what I lost,

I swear I saw his pretty face, His image at our last embrace,

My tears are burning with sudden frost.

My weary mind turns back the time, Feeling those youthful passions,

Life is a holy pantomime,

A sacred mountain hard to climb without love and persuasion.

Life is but a song life is but a dream, Life is but a shadow life is but a vapor, A love story, a romantic theme

Two lovers floating through the stream, Two colors on a piece of paper.

Life is short

I came to life, to live and stay Born on a glorious summer day I thought I was a King, a Lord

Without a scepter, without a sword I step barefooted on the flowers

I realize I have no powers

I walk barefooted on the grass With my half-empty crystal glass I step barefooted on the leaves

I smell the tears as forest grieves I walk barefooted on the snow

I realize that life's a show

I'm dressed in black, my shoes are on My summer nights are forever gone

I knew it's coming, but still deep down I thought I have another dawn

I
am a Lighthouse,

proud and tall, ignoring all the

waves. Inside the chambers of my soul is peace.

I do not care how badly the stormy sea behaves, His songs of love and

mercies never cease. My Keeper helps me daily, my Light is always on, my
eyes have seen

the glory of the resurrected Lord. In the darkest hour, right before the dawn,
the mighty

storm is silent at His majestic Word. I warn so many ships at sea of the great
danger, I show the Light,

the safety to the port, I guide them to The One born in a manger, to the

Truth, the Way, the Life, the strongest Fort,

I am a Lighthouse standing on the Rock of Ages,

The Light for all that hopelessly roam, Hope in all

the storm that rages, I safely lead the sailors to the Home.

Longing for

I am longing for the blue skies, for the stars of hope shining.

I am longing for the tears in the garden, for Your sweet whisper that comfort.

I longing for Your steps, slowly coming to my door.

I am longing for the sunrise, for warm rays full of light.

I am longing for the soft and sweet perfume of the flowers, For Love's fire from my first song.

I am longing for my dear and beautiful Bridegroom, who is coming!

I am longing for the old, holy altar,

for the Sacrifice that brings so much joy.

I am longing for all that without merit, I received as a gift. I am longing for the comfort and the amazing Grace.

I am longing for Heaven; I am longing for Eternity!

I am longing for the old, good peoples, for all our loved ones who went Home.

I am longing for the last trumpet's sound.

I am longing for white clothes, for the crown. I am longing for Jesus; I miss Him so much!

Lost Without You

Lost, wandering the dark paths of my empty soul, Suspended between earth and paradise,

With this sharp pain and dreams beyond my control, My thoughts of you like silent stars arise,

The only light I see it's in your eyes,

The only sound I hear is from your laughter, and from the love's arrow that flies and flies, for our lost love chasing after.

Why are you hiding now, my love? Or maybe you are yet unborn?

I'm mourning silently like a deep hurt dove, There are no roses without a thorn.

I thought I could survive alone, But I am lost forever without you,

I am like a cold, gray, broken stone, Come back to me, let's start anew.

Love and Respect

In our "small group" we are learning, How to give, not to expect,

How daily to be more loving, How daily to show respect?!

If, some words you heard, were hurtful, Stop and think; what can you do?

Don't be caught in the "crazy cycle" You have the answer deep in you.

Show that you are more mature, There's a law; Cause and Effect Even if you are… "not sure"

Show your husband more respect!

If at work… had a bad day, Or your team today is losing, Make the first step anyway,

You can always be more loving!

The true Love cannot be priced, And you'll have a happy life,

Yes, you know the Love of Christ, Show that Love to your sweet wife!

She might be a weaker vessel,

She might look at word through "pink" But she's the Holly Spirit Temple,

You should love her… don't you think?!

If Your husband seems so wrong,

Because he looks at the world through "blue", He's not "singing the same song"

He's not wrong just different… it's true!

When your wife wants you… to stay, to have a talking face-to-face,

It's not easy, brother! Pray! Show your wife a little grace!

If the problem is not the problem, And you're angry and confused, Don't wait until you hit the bottom, Patiently try to "defuse".

Understand your husband need,

Appreciate his heart desires to provide, manage and lead,

And you'll start in him new "fires".

Thank him for his work each day,

He feels respected when "Conquest!" Initiate sometimes… "the play",

Tell him that he is… the best!

Life in two is a blessed road, But frustrations came our way, We are learning to decode, How to act, and… what to say.

We are made in His own image, Husband-Wife the perfect couple, By His Grace we have no limits, Pink and Blue together Purple.

Inspired by the book "Love & Respect: The Love She Most Desires; The Respect He Desperately Needs" by Emerson Eggerichs

Love-Cinquain

Love Patient, kind

Believing, hoping, enduring Rejoicing with the truth God

Me and my Violin

I'm playing my soul for the twinkling stars,

My song is eternal because the soul of music cannot die, I'm not afraid to show my scars,

I'm not ashamed to cry.

The bow dances the tango on strings, My fingers are partners on the ring,

We are lost between winters and springs, We are lost between peasants and kings.

She's not a Stradivarius, I'm not a Paganini, But we're playing like there's no tomorrow,

And flying through the stars, we're free of any darkness, pain, or sorrow.

Memories

blossom of red fires

the graceful poppies dancing fields of love and hope unfolding old memories

as history passes by

Mother

You held me in your arms for the first time, Warm tears were rolling down on your cheek,

Drops of happiness betrayed your infinite excitement, Our two hearts in one then began to beat.

I was safe I was not afraid, Because I felt your love for me,

I understood right then that you are my Mom,

And I knew that for how long I will live, my Mom you'll be.

So many late nights you watched over me Whispering with love… "You'll be fine!" You gave me comfort in pain and sorrow, You were always by my side.

You were there with me when I took the first step, You have inspired me with your power and will,

I felt in your voice, eternal love,

You taught me when to walk and when to stay still.

You walked with me on my first day of school,

The first book that we read together, it's now long past, With love and tender, you corrected my mistakes,

I still remember how you told me; You're the best!

You taught me to say, what I think and what I feel, You told me never, never to lie,

And to live daily for Jesus,

Without any fear, always to watch the sky.

You taught me to comfort others with love, And to spread the Light, all around me, You told me that I am a child of God,

You taught me to believe in Eternity!

So many precious things you planted in me, Today, I thank Jesus, Mother for You,

You gave me life and taught me how to live it, Today, tomorrow, always Mother I Love You.

My Great Red Knight

The sun is waiting at the door, Ready to kiss again the shore

Red-golden cloth the old king wore, Like none before, like none before.

I'm amazed at this great beauty Rays of sunshine are so cutie Fearful waves return to duty, It's all for me, It's all for me.

I wish to stay here all my life,

To make the sand my bed at night, Forever be with him unite,

My great Red Knight, My great Red Knight!

My Harp

I play my harp for stars and moon, I feel I sing with them in tune,

I play for the mountains, for the sea, I'm playing my soul, and I am free.

I play my pains I play my sorrows,

I play my hopes my sweet tomorrows,

I play for the sun, watching from above, I play my laughter, and I play my love.

I play with passion, simple chords, I cry to heaven, without words, She is my fist, my iron rod,

She is my tear, my voice to God.

My King from Fairyland

"A hundred hearts would be too few, " Oceans and seas are not enough,

to carry all my love for you.

To hold my love would be so tough!

Each morning when I see your smile, And when I look into your eyes,

It's like the day I walked the aisle, I see the stars lighting the skies.

Day after day I hold your hand, I walk with you year after year, You are my King from Fairyland,

And heaven starts for us right here.

Your every hug, your every kiss, A precious gift, eternal bliss.

My Romanian Language

Sweet, melodious there's no other like my language in this world, From the lips of my grandmother, every word is shining pearled.

It is born straight from the Light, Sunrise over the Black Sea,

Just to hear it it's a delight,

Oh, how great's my love for thee!

My Romanian language, a treasure Safely kept inside my soul,

Then released with grace and leisure, Golden words that made me whole.

You can hear it in the leaves, when you walk with Eminescu, In the secret of the breeze, Trying lovely to impress you.

It is there in melodies,

In the waves of the Danube In Enescu's rhapsodies

I can hear it, so can you.

It is there in poetry, Written in book after book, Our language molded me, Blaga, Goga, and Cosbuc.

If you carefully listen,

If you have the time and patience, I am sure you too can hear it,

At "The Table of Silence"

At "The Endless Column" With Brancusi dreaming along Our language so solemn

Like an old, enchanted gong.

In the mountains and the valleys, In the rivers in the springs,

In the meadows and green alleys, Unseen angels, touching strings.

Is the language of the songs, Shepherds playing for their sheep, Is a sound where love belongs, Mama's singing you to sleep.

My Little Angel

Your eyes - pure reflection of heaven, The love of God, shining through your hair.

My Queen from God above

A hundred hearts would be too few, Oceans and seas are not enough,

to carry all my love for you.

To hold the love would be so tough!

Each morning when I see your smile, And when I look into your eyes,

It's like the day I walked the aisle, I see the stars lighting the skies.

You are the only one I love,

I walk with you year after year,

You are my Queen from God above, And heaven starts for us right here.

Your every hug, your every kiss, A precious gift, eternal bliss.

My Wife, My Best Friend

I'm blessed to have you in my life

Your care fills up my days with pleasure, I'm thankful that you are my wife,

Your love for me, I treasure!

We walked together one more mile With you the darkest days are sunny You bring me joy with your sweet smile You'll always be my best friend, honey!

New King's Birth

Millions of lights exploded in the night,

The pine tree smiles covered in the snow so white, And all the stars descended to the earth,

To see the humble New King's birth.

Opportunity

walking on water

the biggest faith on the storm opportunity

Option

With my soul saddened by a great burden, Burden bearing, heavy-hearted and hurting,

Hurting others, it's not an option, Option test control my emotion,

Emotion controllers can turn hate to love, Love is a gift that comes from above,

Above all things, it is a delicate, beautiful flower, Flower seeds once planted in your heart gives power,

Power to conquer life like a child, Child of God with Him reconciled.

Wrap Around Poem- each line begins with the last word of the previous line.

Passion-Cinquain

Passion beautiful flower that never dies

the pure essence of life Love

Pearl

gone through some changes got my beauty from the pain little precious pearl

Perception

I walk barefooted in my cage a captive of my hate and rage,

or maybe I just walk barefooted on the grass, with my half-empty crystal glass?

I still don't know which one is true? The sky is gray, the sky is blue?

I just don't know. What do you think? Life is dark, life is pink?

I'm free in prison or a slave outside, We all are going on this ride…

For me, I am the one who should decide.

Perspective

The Carpenter with a small chisel, Carves you- the old and knotted trunk,
He's adding value but for you is a riddle, Feeling the pain in tears you sunk.

The Potter has you- his clay on the wheel, His touch transforms you every hour,

Going through fire… pain again, just pain you feel, But soon you'll be a vase for the beautiful flowers.

The Doctor often cuts out cancer all around, He cleanses with the patience all the bleeding, You can look at the scar and see the wound, Or you can look and see the healing!

Planted by the Streams of Water

Planted by the streams of water, Producing fruits of love and hope, A child of The Heavenly Father,

By His Grace, you'll always prosper, Help and goodness you will offer, You are a tree with a holy scope.

Poet's Thoughts

My thoughts and words fly like a bow, who carries the song,

on the violin strings in the world's symphony.

Prayer Psalm 119: 114-117

You are my hiding place, You are my shield,

You cover me with grace,

You are my armor on the battlefield.

Depart from me, evildoers,

That I may observe the commandments of my God, Depart from me, you, sinful tumors,

I trust in King's iron rod.

Sustain me, as You promised, You are my hope, I trust in You,

Everything that I've accomplished, It's from Your hands, I know it's true.

Uphold me that I may be safe, And I'll rejoice on Your decrees, I will be strong… never afraid,

Listen to my humble prayer… please!

Psalm 19:1-6

Heavens declared the glory of You, Lord Without metaphors, without a rhyme, When only You were there, The Word, Before the distance, space, or time.

The skies proclaim Your awesome work, Night after night reveal Your knowledge, The sun wakes up conquering dark, Riding the skies to sunset, solemn!

Psalm 20

When the day of trouble comes, May all your questions be answered, May The Lord fulfill your plans,

May all your offerings be remembered.

May He grant your heart's desire, Help from heaven He will send, He, The One, clothed in fire,

With His saving, mighty hand,

We shout over Your salvation, Full of joy like river's streams, Because The Lord fulfill petitions,

All our "wants" and all our dreams.

Some trust in horses some in chariots, But we trust Lord's name and fight, They collapse and fall like puppets, But we rise and stand upright.

Psalm 91

Lord, You are my dwelling place, You're my God in whom I trust, I am Yours only by Grace,

And by Grace, You see me just

In all my ways Your angels guard me, They will lead me hand in hand,

In the shadow of The Almighty, The safest place where I will stand,

There's no stone to harm my feet, All the lions only roar,

I will never taste defeat, Victory's forever Yours!

I found peace under Your wings, You're my refuge and my fortress, There are no evils and nothings, That can ever separate us.

In the night I'll fear not, the terror, A thousand may fall at my side,

I'll fear not by day, no arrow, Nor ten thousand at my right.

You are never overdue, When I call upon You Name,

Because Your promises are true, Yesterday, today, the same!

You are Bread for my starvation, Water for my thirsty soul,

You're The Life and my Salvation, I will praise You and adore!

Red Poppies

Born of the blood of heroes shed,

They are watching devoted near the graves, Dressing up the altar of those who now are dead, Dancing free in the wind, no longer slaves!

Like the flames of fire flooding the fields again, With their fragile bodies adorning the earth,

A sweet perfume in the summer's rain,

A place of hope, a place for the new birth,

With their red tears, the fields are watered and, even though they are still sad, they sing With their heart exhausted, shattered,

After any winter is always coming spring!

Red Roses of Love

I kneel at the rugged cross,

and through tears, I ask God for forgiveness, The dried blood from the old tree,

became beautiful red roses of Love.

Red, White, and Blue

I keep proudly in my heart forever these three colors,

The red, white, and blue, are always brightening my summer, Our flag is flying high in the clear sky,

We celebrate the fourth of July,

The sun shining in the morning is the RED,

The sacrifice for our freedom, the crimson bloodshed, The greatness, the courage, the sacred fire burning, The only old covenant I believe in,

The WHITE stripes of purity and innocence, The stars of dreams, unity, and confidence, So many men and women now safely resting, The Hand of God pouring His blessings.

The BLUE skies and the oceans tenacity, perseverance, Persistence, justice, and endurance,

The trust, the confidence, the truth, and faith, America the Beautiful, America the Great.

I keep proudly in my heart forever these three colors,

The red, white, and blue, are always brightening my summer, Our flag is flying high in the clear sky,

We celebrate the fourth of July.

Ring of fire

My love for you, inside the circle, It's like a ring of fire, burning, Strong, pure and kind, eternal, Each day, each night and morning.

The flame we started, goes and goes, It's shining in my heart and glows, My love for you forever grow, Abundantly, like rivers flow.

My love for you is big like oceans, The waves of love will never end, It's like a sea, stirring emotions,

You are my love, my wife, my friend!

My love for you, words can't describe They are too small, so I stand still,

-My heart is trembling deep inside- I love you now, I always will!

A Rose

If I were a tear
I would bathe naked in your
eyes, in the ocean of your pure love,
if I were a smile, I would rest happily in the corner
of your lips, holding to that place forever. If I were a flower,
I would bloom in your chestnut, curly hair gently touching your
velvety white cheek. If I were a wave, I would bring you pearls
from the bottom of the ocean, and if I were the breeze, I
would whisper slowly, in the coolness of the morning,
I Love You! If I were a composer, I would
write musical notes in a bouquet, and
I would lay it down at your feet in
a beautiful song, if I
were a painter, I would
paint on the canvas, red butterfly
the colors of love, if I could fly, I would pick up
for you a bunch of shining stars, and I would make
the sunrise a special gift for you in the morning,
I would put the rainbow at your feet, and I would shout
out my love to you from the top of the mountains in the echo.
But I soak my pen in love and on the white paper
of my pure heart, I sign with red;

I Love You!

I hold you

in my arms,

full of happiness,

once again and

I give you

a rose,

together with

my whole life

forever,

my love!

Marius Alexandru

Salvation Acrostic

Surely, He hath borne our griefs, **A**nd our sorrows He hath carried, **L**oving us, murderers and thieves, **V**alues He hath saw in us,

All we have gone astray, like sheep

Turning each of us to our ways, **I** was putting Him on the cross, **O**ur sins, our transgressions

Not His, was upon Him, the chastisement of our peace.

Saxophone

Sounds of mystery escaped from your wide-opened mouth, are flying among stars, creating a melody.

Angels, drunken by such beautiful songs are dancing, regretting that they are not humans to be able

to touch your body, with their wings,

regretting that they cannot absorb the sounds from your lips,

before the melody of love and sadness is lost forever among the stars.

Searching for Love

I was searching for love in gardens with so many flowers, I thought I could find it in the scent of lilies and roses,

I spent thousands and thousands of hours, So much time wasted in the wrong encloses.

I could swear that I heard the love in the beautiful nightingale's song, and that I saw it on the many colors of the rainbow,

I was looking and looking all summer long,

I was searching for love every valley and mountain, every path every row.

I was chasing red, green and yellow butterflies, Hoping to fulfill my vivid dreams,

I was searching for love in the oceans and skies,

In the dreary wilderness, in the rivers and streams.

I was searching for love in the stars at night,

In the golden dust of the moon sifting through the earth,

I was searching for love at dawn, at the start of morning twilight, In the drops of the rain, in the wind carrying youthful mirth.

I was searching for love I was blind I couldn't see her beauty, her soul brought me a happy glow, True love was waiting patiently next to me,

I found my love, and I never let go.

September 11th

One white dove flew free over the blue sky, that morning in September,

as the giants of glass, marble and steel stood high, under the sunrays, never backing down, and surrender.

They were watching over the bustling city, not knowing that it will be their last breath,

when the flames of fanaticism full of sin, so dirty brought with them pain, sorrow, and death.

So many innocent souls died that day, But the black monster has no victory, We miss our loved ones, cry and pray,

Hope, Freedom, Love, Faith forever alive will be!

From our sad hearts, tears still flow, And we remember them each hour,

Their memories, we'll never let them go,

To their grave humbly today, we bring a flower.

She always had a special way

She always had a special way of showing her great love.

Her love for me I miss today, sweet blessings from above.

The greatest love, wings of the dove, There's nothing like my mother's love,

The greatest love the greatest love

The only love I will speak of.

She always had a special way when held me in her arms.

The safest place I want to stay A place of magic charms.

I miss my Mom, I always will

She's in God's arms, she passed the "hill" I miss my Mom

I miss my Mom

I hear her songs in late nights still.

She always had a special way when kissed my cheeks at night.

I miss her more, and more each day, I see her in The Light.

We'll meet again, soon I'll be "free", Together we'll walk by The Sea.

We'll meet again we'll meet again

A few more years, just wait for me. (A Trijan Refrain)

She is the Spring

She is the shore,

I am the wind, the wave, I am a snowdrop, She is the Spring.

Silence-Cinquain

Silence Emotional, unchanging Mute, quiet, stillness The calmness of the
soul

Peace

Soft Emotion

Soft emotion,

Sad and wounded, broken-hearted, On the bottom of the ocean,

My love is long departed, Just another Oyster-Girl.

In my heart has born a pearl.

Something Magic

I look at you early in the morning, There is something magic in your smile, The fire from your eyes is burning,

I sit and melt there for a while.

Night after night,

you bury me in happiness, with your whispers of love, A little touch of tenderness,

The moon is smiling from above.

I'm awake, I'm dreaming?

Is this my life, my love affair? Thousands of silver stars are rising, in your shining, chestnut hair.

Happy, I soften my pen in sun's drops, and I write with red everlasting verses, The rain, ah the rain finally stops, Enough, enough with this rehearses.

I hear the ocean I marvel at the sailing ships, There is something magic in your smile,

There is something magic in your kisses, in your lips, I think I'll rest here for a while.

Spring's Sonnet

The golden dust of the sad moon, Sifts musical notes all around,

I listen to this simple tune,

Amazing Grace, how sweet the sound.

White angels play the violin,

The yellow birds sing a new song, The party's on, the fun begins, Red flowers smiling, come along.

Blue butterflies dancing with me,

Old stars come down to kiss the earth, New silver bells ring… Victory!

Snowdrops announce the new Spring birth.

Cherry blossom rise in splendor, As the winter slow surrender!

Spring Sunrise

strands of golden light flowery meadow singing a dance of fresh scents

Spring

tears turned into dew

on the still unborn green grass, cherry blossom dance

Steel Giants

All the bright, bright city lights, Extinguished one by one,

I watched in awe the city sights, A day just had begun.

Steel giants with cold eyes never sleep in this town, Looking up they proudly rise,

Wearing their dark, old, rusted crown.

Success

so, what success is? prosperity, affluence? can it be measured?

success is your peace of mind, knowing that you did your best!

Summer

ocean's salty tears drops of pleasure for my soul

ice cream sundae cones

Sunrise Paints the Sky

sunrise paints the sky

yet, sometimes we don't see it look deep inside you

there's a ray of hope right there unveil it an let it shine

Tears

I pray in vain for your sweet tears, alone and sad, in pain and tears.

I see your eyes in stars at night,

From this great sight, I gain just tears.

Forever for our love, I fight,

To see your smile, to kiss your tears.

I always did by you what's right, Why, why my love ended in tears?

Your pretty lips that's what I'll miss, Your rosy cheeks, your joyful tears.

I feel in dreams your touch of bliss, Short nights of pleasures, days of tears.

Without you, love is dark abyss, Life is a cold river of tears.

Marius promises you this;

I love you until I melt in tears. (A traditional Ghazal)

The Black Swan

Sun rays come down to kiss the earth at dawn, snowdrops announce the birth of the new Spring, On the world's scene appears the sad Black Swan.

The Bow Danced on The Strings

My soul reached for the stars

as the bow danced on the strings, Soothing balsam for my scars, Freedom, mysterious wanderings.

I flew with angels through the clouds, No more pain and no more fears,

Just us and the music, no cheering crowds, Calmness and happy tears.

My heart was in such awe, but I don't know why I cried,

Maybe was the love's and music's law, Freedom for my feelings caged inside.

The Child of The-Most-High!

I am like a snowflake descending from-the-sky, A game of small crystals in dance passing by, My life is a moment, a second in Time,

A breath, then a smile… and soon I will die.

I am like the grass, drying slow, on the fields, Without the protection, no armor, nor shields, I'll soon be forgotten, like an old broken string, Until a reborn one is coming in Spring.

I am like a small light, in the deepest abyss, But soon I'll be feeling the Sun's tender kiss, I am like the millions of stars in the sky,

But only my name is; The Child of The-Most-High!

The Christmas Tree

The bright star on top,

Many silver ornaments, Peace on Earth and confidence,

The lights are shining, calm and... silence. Silent night, Holy night, all is calm all is bright.

Christ the Savior is born!

The Day, The Queen of Light

When stillness lies unbroken in the middle of the night, I open my eyes slowly and look up to the sky,

I pray for a song, a sign, something... a beam of light, I pray that you can hear my silent cry.

With a heavy hand, moonlight draws an obscure mask, Hiding everything that is there to see,

Angry that I dare to pray and cry and ask, Angry that I want to fly, to be free.

Poised recklessly, each frame of time halted, The eternity died in that cursed night,

I felt alone, unloved, unwanted,

But suddenly she's there, The Day, The Queen of Light.

She watched the summer sky explode without any fear, The moon is lost forever on the other side,

A song of hope broke the silence, I can hear, The Day has risen and the night has died.

The Dream

The blaze of fires lighting the scene again, Calls you out to a new adventure,

With the window open you can hear the rain, A cup of eternal love and pleasure.

Barefoot, you are dancing in the gentle, idle wind, holding hands with unseen angels,

A romantic waltz, a joyful bind,

A blessing for the eyes of strangers.

Bathed in the brilliant, colored rays, Your smile gives us hope and confidence In a better world for the future days,

A world of love and innocence.

A broken glass in the middle of the night, The music suddenly disappeared,

And everything is gone in the light, It was a dream, just as I feared.

The Great Anthem

Through the old oak trees The wind whistle, soft, a song

Leaves are dancing, falling free With some drops of rain along.

In green pastures cows are happy, Flowers bloom in my old garden, A thousand colors now we see,

As life in summer started.

Puffy clouds are dancing pairs How I wish to dance with them

-I just need a set of stairs- And I'll join the great anthem!

The Hand of God

The Hand of God upon our Earth Mirroring His divine Face

All that we are and all our worth His Mercies, Love, and Grace

The Heaven Within Us

I do not know if in some magic night the heaven opens and the fairies descend to us to give perfume to the flowers, to bring us wealth and fertility or to give healing power to the plants?

I know that for us the heaven was opened once and for all, and remains open to any prayer raised with faith at dawn, to every song of praises with joy in the middle of the day, or to every cry and tears sometimes in the darkest nights.

I know that He came down to us, The Son of God, gave His Life for us, gave color and perfume to the flowers, brought liberation, freedom, healing, peace. He was reconciling the world to Himself.

The heaven is eternally open for us, even more, we are carrying the heaven within us.

When we say a word of encouragement when we erase a tear when we cry with those crying when we spread around smiles when we help when we forgive when we love... we open heaven for others... the heaven within us.

The Life of the Poet

The lyrics are the tender whispers of love...

Poetry is the life of the poet, his soul, his imprint, a journey, a flight, a trail on the sheet of life. I write because I live.

The Light Under the Old-fashioned Coat

Time forgives no mortal soul,

but my soul is not mortal, and time for me is eternity.

Let it not deceive you, this ruin, my old body, a coat that is worthless.

Look carefully, look at the light

under the old-fashioned coat and see the splendor!

The Light

The pot, where I kept so carefully, for so long, hidden, the light, has broken,
And pieces of clay, wrapped in pure gold, now shine scattered in the night.

The Light, finally free, has been divided into thousands and thousands of
rays, into millions of whispers. A splash of Grace, dripped on my dirty head
and under the Light, for the first time clearly, I saw my guilt.

The Magical Night and Morning

It's a magical night in the old garden, and it's all a profound mystery,

We search continuously for God's pardon, This is the path of our history.

Slowly, descending from the stars, The King opens the gate of heaven,

Leaving the Light, He wrapped Himself in scars, And all of us can be forgiven.

It's raining blessings on the earth, The air tremble with songs,

The Star is shining at His birth, All glories to Him alone belongs.

The sounds of Love and Grace in a melody, Forever torn in two the Holly Curtain,

The earth and heaven are in harmony, It's a magical night in the old garden.

The Lamb has died, The King has risen, We tasted The Life, and that is certain, We are free at last, no chains, no prison It's a magical morning in the old garden.

The Mime

So many emotions without a single word You pour your soul on life table
Trying to make a better world Although we live a classic fable

The Most Beautiful Autumn in My Life

The most beautiful Autumn in my life,

End of October, somewhere far away in my memory,

You came down from heaven like a ray of light, like a star, And you have put in my soul a new, unique, love.

It was something special that I didn't know before A feeling I cannot describe,

It was a different love, the father's love,

Something I just dreamed about in my boldest fantasy.

Whispers of angels were your crying sounds, Every smile was like broken from Paradise,

I saw the sun in your shining eyes,

The love from my heart, I promised you forever!

The first words you uttered with such cuteness I will keep them forever framed in my soul,

In the universe the most beautiful song, The most expensive gemstones.

And later when I was letting go of your hand, You took the first steps. I was suffocating.

You were as a Fairy from the most beautiful stories, dancing as a beginner girl in a play.

The sand in the hourglass runs too fast, I'm thanking God for sending you my way, You are an angel in my life,

You will be forever, my little girl.

The Old Cello-Welcomed Acrostic

Welcomed to play what they compose,

Eager to be first, the best

Lost in tunes, in the highs and the lows,

Crying to my rusty strings to rest, **O**h, I'm torn and smeared, unhappy
Maybe I'm destined for weakness,

Every time I play my roles, I grew sappy,

Do I, the old cello, lost my greatness?

The Old Piano

The old and sad piano is sitting in the empty room waiting for the hands of love to touch his dusty keys, waiting for her beauty, for her soul to bloom,

With the window open he can hear the ocean, feel the breeze,

He imagines her long, delicate fingers sliding left and right, caressing him with a great passion,

Her eyes are smiling, glowing bright, There is power in her intimate persuasion.

She enters the room shrouded in mystery,

And once again they are united in a song of love, The musical notes are flying rewriting history, The stars are dancing with the angels from above.

Comforting melody, rage, agony, pain, and tragedy, Crying, laughter, black and white, low and high,

Is this a dream, she's touching me, it's reality? The ocean swallows all his tears,

the song lost into the sky.

The Old White Knight

I am looking from the shore, How the sun is born again, Silent, gratefully, I adore… Mixed colors, blue-red stain!

I'm amazed at this great beauty And my soul is full of light

Happy sunshine dances through me My hair changed in golden-bright.

I wish to stay here all my life, Make the sand my bed at night, Here I feel again alive,

Me, the brave, new…..."Old White Knight"!

The One

When you're hurt looking for answers, And your tears like rivers flow,

When you're tired of taking chances, When you don't know where to go,

He, The One has all the answers, He'll erase your doubts and fears, He will give you brand new chances, He will wipe away your tears!

The Power of Perception

I walk barefooted in my cage, a captive of my hate and rage,

or maybe I just walk barefooted on the grass, with my half-empty crystal glass?

I just don't know which one is true? The sky is gray or the sky is blue?

I just don't know? What do you think? Life is dark or life is pink?

I'm free in prison, or a slave outside? We all are going on this ride.

For me, I am the one who should decide.

This beautiful world

This beautiful world is all but mine, White angels, butterflies, and birds, Dancing and singing so divine,

A melody with magic notes and words.

Surrounded by the crystal seas,

I feel the breeze kissing my cheeks,

The golden leaves falling from the trees, This is all mine it's how Love speaks.

From the top of the mountains,

I touch the sky with my right-wing, So many blessings, I quit counting, I knell down and happy… I sing.

Together

We can find each other on the thick mist of troubles, We can discover the beauty of our faces all again, Despite our fears, our pains, despite our struggles, Soon we will dance, together, hand in hand in the rain.

We miss the handshakes, the hugs, but we are not lost, We are crying, but we will never forget to smile,

We'll pay the price we'll pay the cost,

We'll be coming back to "happy" in just a little while.

We never lost the faith, the hope, the love, He is the same, yesterday, today, and forever, The clouds might be gray-dark today above, But we will pass through the storms together.

Trapped

Walking in the world of gray and black,

lost in my thoughts, a stranger that nobody sees, I made friends with some old, sad trees,

Hoping for help to get my way back.

I could hear the silence crying out loud, And the rain was so cold and strange,

I wished in secret for a mysterious change, I felt so alone in this silent, vast crowd.

Whispers, shadows, unseen angels… The full moon and broken stars,

The forest wear so many scars,

I am a stranger in the arms of strangers.

Trapped between my wish to go home, to read a book in front of my fireplace, and to my need to kiss the forest face, I choose to pray, cry, and free to roam.

inspired by the poem "Padure Arsa" by Nichita Stanescu

True Love

True love never dies.

Like a flame, it's always burning.

True love consumes because it sacrifices. True love suffers because it forgives.

True love hurts because it trusts.

True love never dies because true love always believes.

Unrequited Love

If I were the sky

I would wait for you to rise,

to feel your soft and tender lips kissing my eyes,

but I'm just the earth, and when you rise

I feel the pain,

I turn to dust and cry.

Whishes

I want to cry with them that cry,

And to relieve through love their pain, To learn together again how to fly,

To see the shining stars across the sky, The suffering is not in vain!

I want to rejoice with them that rejoice, And smiles to offer all around,

To learn that happiness's a choice, Encouragement to be in my voice, Power of love in every sound!

I want to be silent with them that are silent, To hear their whisper like a sunset,

To show my love by being quiet, A Love that no one can deny it, A Love that no one can forget!

I want to sing with them that sing, To put Your Love into my rhymes, Praises to You to bring in everything, Forever You're my Lord and King,

Yesterday, today, tomorrow in the future times!

White Snowdrop

Planted in God's garden,

I am a snowdrop, full of grace

I am clean, my sins been pardoned, A new creation in this new place.

I'm born to whisper Spring is here, A new beginning for the world, Look all to me and do not fear,

I am a white snowdrop for the Lord!

Wildflowers

Blossoms of fire are flooding the fields again, Adorning the earth with their suave bodies, A subtle perfume in the summer's rain,

A cup of eternal love for all the ladies.

Slowly dancing in the gentle, idle wind, Holding hands with unseen angels,

A romantic waltz, a joyful bind,

A blessing for the eyes of strangers.

Bathed in the brilliant, colored rays, Your smile gives us hope and confidence In a better world for the future days,

A world of love and innocence.

Winter Wonderland

snowflakes in a dream the frozen light is dancing winter wonderland

Yellow Autumn

fluffy silver clouds

the melted sun kisses trees honeydew-gold leaves

You never stopped loving me

You searched for me through dark valleys, You have suffered so much to find me,

I was dirty, hidden in the marshes of sin,

But through Your Love, You saw me like a precious stone, You never stopped loving me.

From the cross You whispered to me;

"Receive the Gift!", "You are saved, My child forever!" Out of the black slag, You raised me with Your Grace, Through Your great Love, You saw me like a pearl,

You never stopped loving me.

You have risen! The death is defeated!

You prepared me a place in heaven with You, And if sometimes, my heart is broken again,

I remember, and my soul starts to sing, You never stopped loving me.

Your Presence

When foaming waters in testing rivers, Disturbed my faith and kept me on the shore, In diseases, in suffering and storms at sea,

You have overwhelmed me with peace and mercy, You were there, present in every wave.

When cold and black shadows, through the valleys of complaints, Often followed me, day after day, hour after hour,

You immediately sent angels to serve me, I felt in my soul God's touches,

You were there with me at every step.

When mountains with high peaks were in my way, And my doubt whispered; You'll never get over them! When I was sad, and alone, heavily burdened,

You smiled secretly at me through flowers and rainbow, You were there with me on the trail.

When in rains with many tears my cheek was wet, When rushed in my life flood after flood,

When despair covered me with fear, You gave me strength, I felt Your Love,

You were there with me, present in every drop.

When the night was dark, and the guilt followed me again, When I felt my friends betrayal,

When the thorns of sin overtook my garden,

You clothed me in Your Grace, You showed me The Light, You were there with me, present in every ray.

You are the same yesterday, today, forever, Eternal, Unchanged, Filled with a holy longing I worship and wait for You,

The Holiday is approaching, and the bells are ringing, It is a new morning, Christ has risen!

You are alive, present in my heart!